-O-
5/13/02

Heart TO Heart

New Poems Inspired by Twentieth-Century American Art

EDITED BY JAN GREENBERG

HARRY N. ABRAMS, INC., PUBLISHERS

To Sandra Jordan

Acknowledgments

I am deeply grateful to all the poets who participated in this project for their enthusiastic and spirited responses. Through e-mail, letters, and telephone conversations, many have become friends of the heart. Special thanks go to David Clewell and Marlene Birkman for their expertise and good humor, to Lynne Greenberg for her scholarly resources, to my agent, George Nicholson, to Barbara Sturman for her colorful design, and to Greenberg Van Doren Gallery and the artists, art resources, galleries, and museums around the country, who cheerfully provided transparencies of the artworks. I also would like to express my appreciation to my stalwart editor Howard Reeves and creative assistant editor Lia Ronnen at Harry N. Abrams, Inc., not only for their encouragement, but also for their thoughtful advice and total involvement in the process of turning an idea into a reality.

Designer: Barbara Sturman

Library of Congress Cataloging-in-Publication Data

Heart to heart : new poems inspired by twentieth century American art / edited by Jan Greenberg.
     p.   cm.
   Summary: A compilation of poems by Americans writing about American art in the twentieth century, including such writers as Nancy Willard, Jane Yolen, and X.J. Kennedy.
  ISBN 0–8109–4386–7
    1. Art, Modern—20th century—Poetry. 2. Art, American—Poetry. 3. American poetry—20th century. [1. Art, American—Poetry. 2. Art, Modern—20th century—Poetry.
3. American poetry—Collections.] I. Greenberg, Jan

  PS595.A75 H43 2001
  811'.6080357—dc21   99–462335

Printed and bound in China

10 9 8 7 6 5 4 3 2

 Harry N. Abrams, Inc.
100 Fifth Avenue
New York, N.Y. 10011
www.abramsbooks.com

Contents

Introduction

I still can picture myself at age ten, racing through the Great Hall of the St. Louis Art Museum with my mother close behind saying, "Slow down." My pulse would quicken when I saw her — *Little Dancer of Fourteen Years,* a bronze sculpture with a net tutu by the French artist Edward Degas. Chin up with a peevish expression, she exuded frustration and painful effort. Not surprisingly, the tales I invented about her echoed my own misadventures in ballet class. My mother, a writer, encouraged me to put these stories down on paper. Of course I didn't do it. In high school, I went to the museum on my own, always stopping to visit the *Little Dancer,* who remained frozen in time. However, the way I perceived her had changed. I began to notice how the artist had used line and form, texture and color, to express the dancer's wonderfully cranky mood. The more I looked, the more I learned. I heard my mother's voice urging, "Write it down." Finally I did. My first poems were inspired by art.

In college I discovered there was a long tradition of poets writing on art, going back to ancient Greece. I read Homer's description of Achilles' shield and John Keats' *Ode on a Grecian Urn.* The list grew. Now in my books on American art, I find that including poetry enriches the text, adds an element of surprise. For what the poet sees in art and puts into words can transform an image, "giving us a sense," says the poet Bobbi Katz, "of entering a magical place," and extending what is often an immediate response into something more lasting and reflective.

These connections between reader and viewer, writer and artist, resulted in this anthology, celebrating the power of art to inspire language. A group of distinguished American poets were invited to choose a twentieth-century American artwork and write a poem stimulated by it. The response was enthusiastic, eliciting not only a variety of voices and visions, but also offering some unexpected perceptions. For example, Nancy Willard says of her choice of the photograph *Horses* by Eric Lindbloom, "I find dreams useful to me as a writer. If I could save a dream, hold it in my hand and study it, I believe it might look like this picture." David Mura's poem on Pacita Abad's painting *How Mali Lost Her Accent* is a poignant reminder of the loss of cultural identity that can follow assimilation in America. Sources for poems vary from dreams to childhood memories, with issues of race or gender, along with reflections of family or place, coming into play. But in each case, the poem is triggered by an encounter with art.

From an abstract painting by Arthur Dove or a sculpture by Charles M. Russell in the first quarter of the century to the post–World War II paintings of Jackson Pollock or Jaune Quick-to-See Smith, American artists have explored the diversity of the American experience. Although they reflect a variety of styles, methods, and materials, the artworks visited here are not intended to be a comprehensive survey of the last hundred years; however, they evoke many of the most important movements in American art. The poems written about these images are like valentines sent from one heart to another. Thus the art is arranged by themes suggested by the poetry, rather than being placed in historical order.

As I read and discussed the poems, four distinct but complimentary motifs seemed to emerge. STORIES includes poems that conjure a memory or tell an anecdote. Jacinto Jesús Cardona remembers himself as a Mexican-American schoolboy, "strapped with satchel and bifocals . . . impressed with the streetwise vibes rippling from a cool bato," similar to the youth so vividly portrayed in César A. Martínez' *Bato Con Khakis.* Prompted by the sculpture *Woman at the Piano* by Elie Nadelman, William Jay Smith transforms the prim lady into a wild, skirt-flying performer carried away by her own playing. Based on the scene illustrated in the artwork, each poet recalls or imagines a story of his or her own.

VOICES contains poems in which the poet steps inside the artwork and assumes the voice of the object or person depicted there. In Angela Johnson's poem on *Tar Beach,* a quilt painting by Faith Ringgold, a child imagines she is floating in the sky looking down at her family's picnic on the roof. In his shaped poem on Andy Warhol's painting of the movie star Marilyn Monroe, David Harrison takes on her persona and wonders which one of the many repeated images is the "real Marilyn." By projecting his or her spirit into the artwork, each poet gets closer to the feeling expressed by the artist.

IMPRESSIONS displays the poets' powers of description as they examine the elements of the artwork and offer vibrant word pictures based on what is contained there. In her poem on Georgia O'Keeffe's painting *Poppy,* Janine Pommy Vega turns to metaphor. Looking at the painting, reading the poem, and looking back again, we spin into the skirts of a flamenco dancer, an image roused by the flower's swirling red petals. Marvin Bell takes us on a stroll through the colorful streets of Paris as he narrates the details of Red Grooms' painting *French Bread.* "I like the painting because it is audacious. It has the dash of a cartoon, the vigor of a peacock, and a fresh take on proportion. After all, if you are the one who walks to the baker each morning to buy bread for the day, you feel ten feet tall." In these poems, the poets do not invent a new story or recall a childhood memory but concentrate on what they see within the frame of the canvas or the form of the sculpture. However, their acts of seeing are not mere descriptions; they move into interpretation, into a space where one work of art calls forth another.

EXPRESSIONS explores aspects of visual form that concern the nature of art and the artist. Naomi Shihab Nye writes of her attraction to

Florine Stettheimer's whimsical canvases. "Her scenes woke me up with their beautifully luscious shapes and colors of flowers and figures, and gave me a deep feeling of closeness with the times in which she lived." As the new century begins, Nye looks back with nostalgia on the vanishing grace of Stettheimer's world. In Donald Finkel's poem on Edward Hopper's *Nighthawks,* the poet considers the artist's use of light and the way it reflects and is reflected in the details of this moody scene of an all-night American diner. Here each poet transfers the artist's considerations of form or light or space into poetic language.

Some poets chose to write in free verse, as well as in such traditional forms as the sonnet or rhymed verse; others experimented with patterns, using repeated lines or parts of speech. Kristine O'Connell George says, "*Fluttering Eyes,* a print by Kiki Smith, haunted me. I wondered: Whose eyes? What were they thinking about? What were their stories? What had they seen? These questions kept repeating themselves in my mind — which is why I chose the pantoum form with its repeating lines." In addition there are several poems about paintings by the same artist, including Edward Hopper, Georgia O'Keeffe, and Joseph Stella, to offer the reader comparisons both to these artists' works as well as to the interesting range of poetic responses.

Whether the words are playful, challenging, tender, mocking, humorous, sad, or sensual, each work of art, seen through the eyes of a poet, helps us look at the world around us with fresh insight. I hope you will take an imaginary walk through this book as if it is a gallery, the pages hung with artworks, and try your own hand at a poem. On Stuart Davis' lively painting *Premiere,* X. J. Kennedy suggests, "Perhaps you can imagine a different story inspired by this painting. Look at the picture long and I think that you too will find it overflowing with possibilities."

— JAN GREENBERG

★ STORIES

Down by the Riverside

DAVE ETTER

Thomas Hart Benton. Down by the Riverside. 1969. Oil on canvas. © T. H. Benton and R. P. Benton Testamentary Trusts/Licensed by VAGA, New York, NY

Uncle Roy
has done it
again. He
has sailed our
bright orange kite
with the long
and fancy
tail into
the summer
sky. He will
soon make it
fly higher
and higher.
My sister
Lucinda
prances on
spongy grass.
Our yellow
dog Barney
barks and barks
his doggie
approval.
Mom and Dad
have seen lots
of orange kites
dance in a
warm breeze. Mom
gulps a cold
drink while Dad
is busy
at the grill
cooking meat.
Both of them
leave us to
our young joy
down by the
riverside.

Woman at the Piano

WILLIAM JAY SMITH

Elie Nadelman. Woman at the Piano. c. 1917.
Wood, stained and painted

When the tall thin lady started to play
the notes flew up and out and away:
like the pink in her cheeks and her dress's loops
they rose in curves, they rolled in hoops
till the chickens flew out of the chicken coops,
the rooster crowed, the donkey brayed,
and the cat meowed.

                She raised her hands,
she lifted her feet.

What was she playing?
                An anthem? A hymn?
Nobody knew, but, oh, it was sweet!

How thin she was, how tall and prim,
                but, oh, how she played!

Everything in you went loose inside
and the world of a sudden became so wide
and open and joyous and free
the fish came flying out of the sea,
the mountains knelt,
                the birds went wild.

The lady smiled:

and all you could do was hold on to your seat
and simply say:

"For heaven's sake, lady, play, play!
For heaven's sake,
                lady,
                    play!"

The Peacock

DEBORAH CHANDRA

The Peacock cries,
he doesn't quack,
or coo,
twitter,
chirp,
or say, "Tu-whit, tu-whoo!"
He cries —
a loud sorrow — so desolate,
the air shrinks back
to make space for it.

But if,
as he unfolds his emerald fan,
his feathers turned
as common as a wren's,
would he be free of his
        parading strut,
and maybe —
make a
soft,
contented,
cluck?

Joseph Stella. **The Peacock**. c. 1919. Pastel on paper

Dream Horses

NANCY WILLARD

When I was thirteen I found two horses.
The shining one calls itself, *Keeper of
    Lights.*
The wild one calls itself, *Never Tame Me.*

Keeper of Lights comes when I call her
from the stable at the end of the world
hung with bridles and bits so soft
a rose might wear them and love
    the journey.

Never Tame Me shies at the sight of
    a saddle,
bare as a wave with her rocking gait
when we gallop on the dark meadows.
The rim of the sea is her fence.

One carries me home, the other
    shadows her
on the slippery trail shifting and
    shaking
where even a river could lose its way

between sleeping and waking.

Eric Lindbloom. **Horses.** 1979. Gelatin silver print

The Bison Returns

TONY JOHNSTON

Charles M. Russell. Standing Buffalo. 1900–1920. Wax, plaster, and paint

Midnight and the world so cold.
The sky is holding snow.
On the stone flank of a buried cave
an old fire-smear awakes
and walks out, down the drifted miles,
down the smothered hills.

It steps into the yard to graze
just as snow begins
falling soundless in a dream
upon the shaggy ghost.
What will I say to keep it here?
What song will I sing?

The Brown Bomber

CAROLE BOSTON WEATHERFORD

William H. Johnson. **Joe Louis and Unidentified Boxer.**
1939–42. Tempera, pen, and ink with pencil on paper

The radio gave folks a ringside seat
to cheer Joe Louis during his prize
    fights;
twenty-three titles and but one
    defeat.
Fans partied past dawn under neon
    lights
as if their own clenched fists had
    struck each blow.
They called Joe the Brown Bomber.
    He attacked
big, bad opponents, threatened old
    Jim Crow
who kept doors closed to hold his
    people back.
He was a secret weapon in a war
to knock out hate. Joe bore a million
    hopes
each time he punched a foe. He was
    a star;
his stage, a mat set off by stakes
    and ropes.
A left hook, a right jab, muscle and
    grace;
Joe danced, and pride glowed on
    every brown face.

Bato Con Khakis

JACINTO JESÚS
CARDONA

Too bold for my mother's blood,
bato was not a household word.
Oh, but to be a bato con khakis
waiting to catch the city bus,

my thin belt exuding attitude,
looking limber in a blue vest,
laid-back in my dark shades.

Alas! I'm the bifocals kid;
cool bato I am not,
but I could spell gelato.
Could I be the bookish bato?

Oh, but to be a bato con khakis
deep in the Hub of South Texas,
blooming among bluebonnets.

César A. Martínez. **Bato Con Khakis**. 1982. Mixed media on paper

Early Sunday Morning

DAN MASTERSON

Edward Hopper. Early Sunday Morning. 1930. Oil on canvas

My big brother & I grew up behind
Three windows over our father's barber
Shop where half-drawn shades painted
Squares of buttery light on the wall
Beside the sink & on the mirror near
The worn end of the corduroy sofa.

We played barefoot stickball with Mongie
Stritt & Potatoes McGowen & Dutch Finn
& if the cobblestones got too hot
We'd send Mongie for his father's stilson
Wrench & open the fireplug crank-nut
& hose caps, the sideways flood splish
Splashing downhill past Cudlip's Candy Store
& around the diner into the schoolyard.

I don't know why the iceman came early
On Sunday mornings, but he did, hauling
50-pound blocks of ice into McGinley's
Before dancing up the outside stairs
With 25-pounders for all the neighbors,
While my brother & I scooped up slivers
Of ice from the wet wooden planks
Of the wagon & fed them to the pull-horse,
Watching him do his own kind of dance,
Happy to be done with his awful thirst.

On muggy nights, we'd climb out our bedroom
Window & go up the fire escape to spread
Double layers of newspapers side by side
On the bubbly tar roof & lie on our backs
Giving new names to old stars & listening
To the Hudson River slap the rocks on its
Way to the Atlantic where soon my brother
Would sail off to war & promise to come back.
He even crossed his heart & hoped to die.

Sit a While

SIV CEDERING

Sit a while.
What do you hear?
A bird? A bus? A baby's cry?
The shouting of a boy?
                    For joy?
Leaves rustling?
    Trains rattling?
        Skateboards rolling?
            A boombox blaring?
A mother calling?
The droning of a car?
                    Or ten —
traveling far, then home again,
    like your thoughts
        as you sit
with nothing much to do but
    contemplating it?

Romare Bearden. **Black Manhattan**. 1969. Collage. © Romare Bearden
Foundation/Licensed by VAGA, New York, NY

Stuart Davis: Premier, 1957

X. J. KENNEDY

With large and swollen bag
    of milk.
She stands, this stabled cow.
Black cat pads in on cushioned
    feet
To raise a loud MEOW.

Now farmer squeezes bag —
    oh, see
The warm white fluid sluice! —
As fat cat begs for any drop
Of creamy new cow juice.

Well fed, cat purrs, one
    hundred per
Cent sound asleep, it seems,
While Sandman sprinkles her
    for free
From his large bag of dreams.

Stuart Davis. Premier. 1957. Oil on canvas. © Estate of Stuart Davis/
Licensed by VAGA, New York, NY

Crommelynck Gate

ROBERT STEWART

My father kept a claw
    hammer in a flowered
    vase
that once belonged to my
    great grandmother.
Its wooden handle in white-
    ceramic rose
blooms, glazed vines, thin
    as Rold Gold Pretzels.
This was the vase I rescued,
last immigrant to arrive
at these two gates

of twisted tools, my arms.
A miracle nothing was
    broken.
At union hall, or church
of the Little Flower, my
    father
drove in the feathery nail
of his own construction:
a word for God, or
    brotherhood,
or what has not been
    mentioned —

how we use the tools
that are given us.
I'd been looking for closet
    auger
in the car trunk, brace
    and bit
and crutch in the rafters.
It was what my father
    had found,
such a beautiful place to
    keep his hammer.

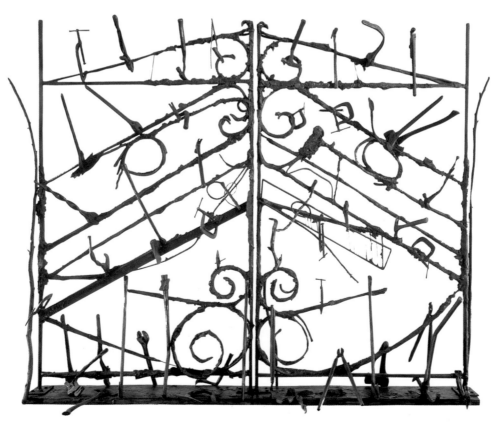

Jim Dine. The Crommelynck Gate with Tools. 1984. Cast bronze with welded appendages

Arthur Dove. **That Red One**. 1944. Oil and wax on canvas

A Word

GARY GILDNER

Give me I said to those round
young faces a round word
and they looked at me
fully puzzled until finally
several cried What do you mean?

I mean I said round round
you know about round
and Oh yes they said but
give us examples!

Okay I said let's have a
square word
square maybe
will lead us to round.

And they groaned
they groaned and they frowned
every one except one
little voice way in the back said
Toast.

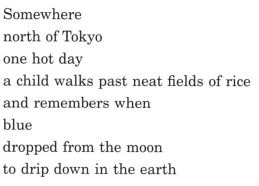

Dropped and Sprung

JANET S. WONG

Somewhere
north of Tokyo
one hot day
a child walks past neat fields of rice
and remembers when
blue
dropped from the moon
to drip down in the earth

while

somewhere
north of Los Angeles
one cold day
a child walks past wild grassy hills
and remembers how
yellow
sprung from the earth
to soak up the sun.

Christo and Jeanne-Claude. The Umbrellas,
Japan — USA. 1984—91. Opposite: Ibaraki, Japan
Site. Above: California Site. © Christo, 1991

George Bellows. **Stag at Sharkey's**. 1909. Oil on canvas

Ringside

RON KOERTGE

It all started when a new teacher held up
this picture and asked, "What's going on here?"
Everybody said how pretty the yellow house
was, the pink blossoms, the blue sky.
I said, "It's creepy. The sidewalk leads
right to the cellar." The teacher beamed
and the McKenzie brothers made fists.

I ran for the library faster than usual.
I asked Miss Wilson for more by the same guy.
She could only find one — *Stag at Sharkey's.*

I looked at that painting every day. I looked
at every inch. I looked until I was at ringside,
until I was the fighter in the modest black
trunks.

When Bobby McKenzie finally caught me
and bloodied my nose, I put my head against
his and hit him with my right and to my surprise
he winced and went down.

"Stag at Sharkey's," I bellowed. He looked
at me like I was crazy, scrambled to his feet,
and ran.

★ VOICES

From Above

ANGELA JOHNSON

Faith Ringgold. Tar Beach. 1988. Acrylic on canvas bordered with printed, painted, quilted, and pieced cloth

When it is a warm time
        in the evening
and my people are
        laughing
and warm
beside me,
it almost feels like
I can fly.
Above the city and
        everything
I know.
— And I am happy in
        the coolness
as I am in the warmth,
because I can fly as
free as I feel
and watch my people
with love
from
above.

Pacita Abad. How Mali Lost Her Accent. 1991. Acrylic, oil, and collage on stitched and padded canvas

Fresh from the Island Angel

DAVID MURA

Father, where is the sea? The surf of my heart?
The girls with their twirling skirts of memory,
Who go down to the waves, soaking their garments.
Whose hearts were white. Whose skin was dark.

(Now I live where these colors are reversed.)
The swells were so blue there. And the nights.
Yes, we there sometimes hated our blackness.
But in secret, in secret we loved it even more.

You tell me our life here is new. And I believe you.
It's just: I believe them too. Their loud loud voices.
On the streets. In my class. On the chalkboards.
In numbers in my notebook. The flag above my desk.

Inside my chest I still hold corridors of sunlight.
Villages where palms and pomegranates and linen blow.
Streets where people simply walk, day by day, into their lives.
The dust beneath their soles. The rain. The mud.

Father, I know I'll forget all this.
I'll be different then.
No longer your angel.
No longer yours.

Martha Graham in "Letter to the World"

LYN LIFSHIN

Barbara Morgan. Martha Graham, Letter to the World. 1940.
Gelatin silver print

"You have so little
time," she writes, "each
instant is so

exciting. At first,
in the early days I was
made fun of. I was

in my long underwear.
I took off my bangles.
We took women
off pointe shoes

I wanted life the way
it is." Her long neck,
her lips dark, like a
young girl's. "Only

dance if you have to.
If you think you want a
family, a home, don't."

Her words, a swirl of
her body, hair pulled
back, her face

wide open

A Provocation

LEE UPTON

Louise Bourgeois. Defiance (Le Defi). 1991. Painted wood, glass, and electric light. Art © Louise Bourgeois/Licensed by VAGA, New York, NY

I don't want to be rearranged.
    Anyway,
there's not much room for things
    to change.

Tip one glass: that's my hand.
I could be rolled away.

I'll stay with you because
you want to look through me.

So many decanters and globes,
and so much almost the same.

Do you want to dust me — or
count my features? Look at
    how many

empty places I take up,
how I'm like a game

in a shooting gallery.
You think I'm a thing —

a cabinet of things easy to
    shatter —
but I'm a person.

Walk quietly around me.

Marisol. The Family. 1962. Painted wood and other materials in three sections. Art ©
Marisol/Licensed by VAGA, New York, NY

Breaking Away from the Family

SUSAN TERRIS

I'm there. See me in yellow? Not the short one
with no visible arms. That's my sister.
I'm the frowning-smiling girl eyeing the family.
See us? Sister, Sister, Mother, Baby. Then Brother,
at his board-like best, standing in too-big overalls
trying to be Papa. We're caught there,
nailed and glued to a door with no house,
a door that won't open. Only my half-laced
boots are real. The rest: flat-tinted,
an odd two dimensional, one-handed girl.

The part of me that's broken away
has grown tall, drives a car, goes to work, lives
in a house with a real door. She's warm
and full-fleshed and dances with boys under
a flower moon. But the splintered girl I was
keeps coming back, returns me here
to stare at Mother's pork sausage fingers,
at her dress with its bear-claw flowers.
Overhead, black scrolls hold her and them
like curved iron bars of a jail insisting:

You may never leave
or change or be part of any family
except this one staring helplessly outward.
Papa will not return.
Brother will not become Papa.
Baby will always be propped in Mother's lap.
Sister will never find her arms.
The five of us will always be
the last picture Papa saw before he went,
a stiff wooden portrait left behind.

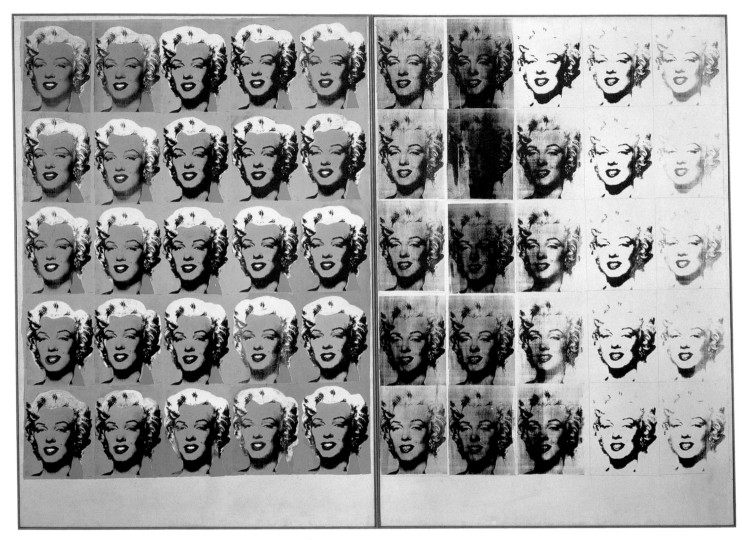

Andy Warhol. Marilyn Diptych. 1962. Synthetic polymer paint and silkscreen ink on canvas

It's Me!

DAVID HARRISON

Hey!

Over here!

It's me!

The real Marilyn!

Shhh!

Don't tell the others!

They don't know they're fakes!

Hey!

Over here!

It's me!

The real Marilyn!

Shhh!

Don't tell the others!

They don't know they're fakes!

Hey!

Over here!

It's me!

y'hear
y'hear it everywhere
gassy in the Halls of State,
shrewd sceptic joshing where the brothers meet
cool, understated underneath the hoop
jabjabjabjabjabjabbering on the phone
unseen ungraspable, but virus on the net —
  America at any moment
       barks and burps and jabberbobbles noises
       hop hip hop from him to you to her to them to me
the land's a hummmmmmmm
        "we hold these truths. . . ."
        "the kid's so cute. . . ."
        "the ump's a bum."

America Talks

PETER F. NEUMEYER

            "a little off the top."

Jacob Lawrence. Barber Shop. 1946. Gouache on paper

Naming

Or, There is no such thing as an Indian

JOY HARJO

Jaune Quick-to-See Smith. Indian, Indio, Indigenous. 1992. Oil and collage on canvas

I call my sisters to dress for the stompdance
As all the little creatures hum and sing
in the thick grass around the grounds.
Lighting bugs are tiny stars
dancing in the river of dusk.
Our stomachs full of meat and frybread
and the talk of aunts and uncles.
Beautiful fire at the center of the dance
and the dusk has been lit.
We lace up our turtle shells so we
can dance into the circle.
And in this spirit world is the grocery
store over the hill, and all the houses
the river, sky and the highway.
We have been here forever
say our mother, our father.
And this is the name we call ourselves
I tell my sisters,
this name that gives our legs the music
to shake the shells
this name that is unspeakable
by those who would disrespect us
a name with power to thread us through
the dark to dawn
a name that leads us faithfully
to the stars.

★
IMPRESSIONS

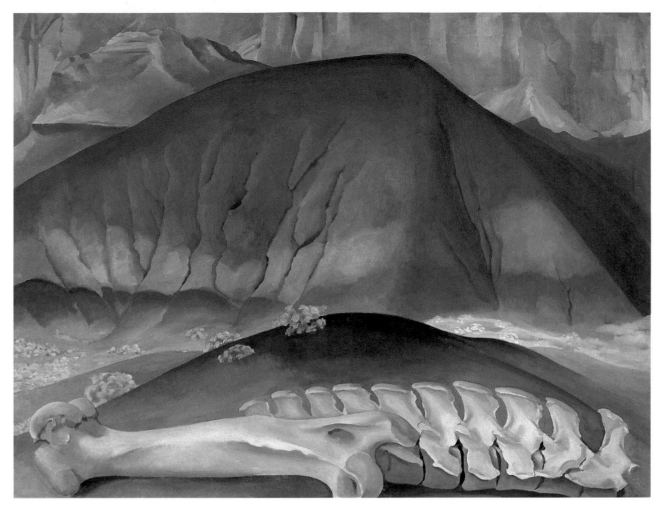

Georgia O'Keeffe. Red Hills and Bones. 1941. Oil on canvas

Red Hills and Bones

LAURA KASISCHKE

Where there are no flowers, everything
    becomes a flower.
Without water, everything turns to water —
    the hills

are red water stirred by a hand, and will
always be. Bright light in the dull bones.
    Like

the ladder
of a spine
laid down
in the desert.
You can climb

to the world you want. You can paint
    the world you see.

On a Windy Wash Day Morn

BRENDA SEABROOKE

Soaked and scrubbed in a round tin tub
with homemade soap
up and down the ribs of a wooden washboard
by hands rubbed red & raw
on a windy wash day morn.

Stiffened with starch, squeezed
and wrung to a twisted laundry rope
then hung on lines to flap

back and forth and snap dry
on a windy wash day morn.

Laid on the lawn like paper cutouts
clean shirts and sheets, towels and skirts
smelling of sun and clouds and wind
wait to be ironed and worn and dirtied
again for another wash day morn.

Grandma Moses. Wash Day. 1945. Oil on masonite

Grant Wood: American Gothic

JANE YOLEN

Grant Wood. American Gothic. 1930. Oil on beaverboard

Do not dwell on the fork,
the brooch at the throat,
the gothic angel wing
of window pointing toward
a well-tended heaven.
Do not become
a farmer counting cows
as if the number of the herd
defines you.
Look behind the eyes,
to see who looks out at you.
We are not what we own.
We own what we would be.

Madinat as Salam

CONSTANCE LEVY

Frank Stella. Madinat as Salam III. 1971. Acrylic on canvas

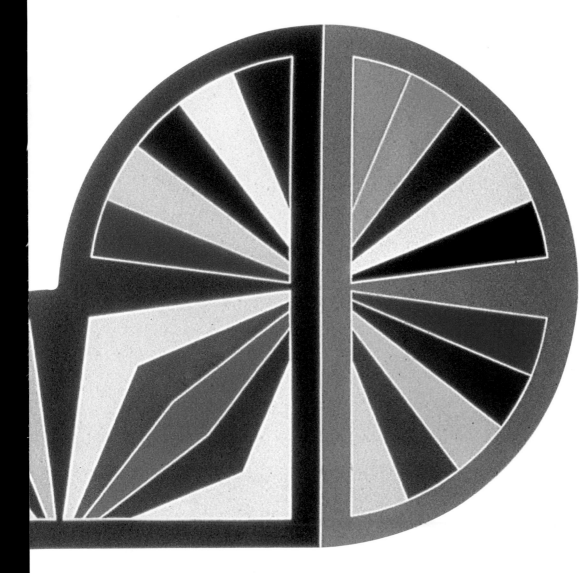

Watch
this top notch
tightrope walk —
It's really hot,

balancing
the twin
colossal wheels,
that are not round
or quite the same,

as colors pulse
like beating hearts
and curves
and angles
tease,

juggling
geometry
inside a frame-less
frame!

Catch this act —
It's cool!

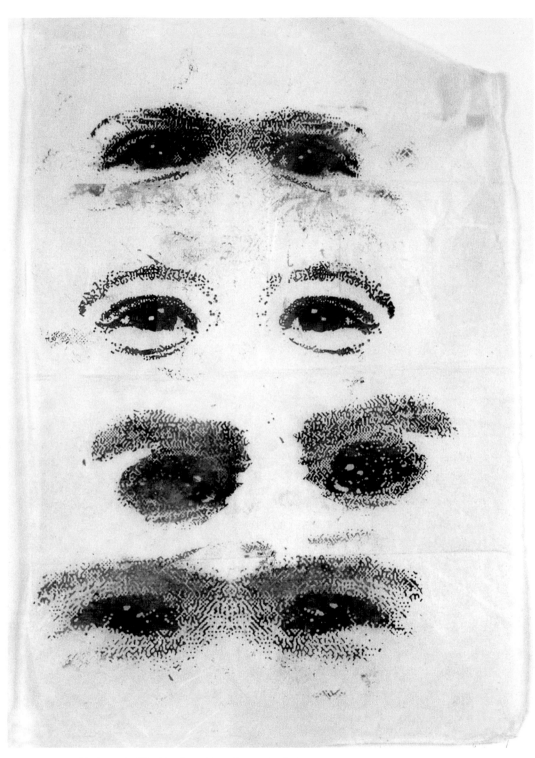

Kiki Smith. Untitled (Fluttering Eyes). 1990. Print

Pantoum for These Eyes

KRISTINE O'CONNELL GEORGE

Let yourself slide under their spell —
these eyes have something to say.
Write the stories these eyes tell,
look deeply, don't look away.

These eyes have something to say.
Come, come meet these eyes.
Look deeply, don't look away,
find their truth, discover their lies.

Come, come meet these eyes,
sketches of shadow, smudge and line.
Find their truth, discover their lies,
look into eyes with faces left behind.

Sketches of shadow, smudge and line,
write the stories these eyes tell,
look into eyes with faces left behind.
Let yourself slide under their spell.

Big French Bread

MARVIN BELL

Today we are up with the sun and down on the street.
A man in blue pants, blue jacket and size twelves
cradles a loaf of bread as long as an oar. The aroma

encircles his head, and the bread's chewy center
steams his hand, and the dark crust,
which resembles a leg that has lain too long in the sun,

crackles like a brown paper sack as he walks.
He loves his bread as the redhead loves the light,
flinging open her shutters. He loves it as the old lady

on the balcony cares for her plants, and the man
with the umbrella his spotted dog, and the young girl
her walks to school and the first class of the day.

He walks with giant strides, holding his bread close,
nestling it in the crook of his arm above the dust
adrift near the street sweeper's long-handled broom.

The woman who buys two baguettes each morning
walks briskly, and a bicyclist peddles past in a hurry,
but we stay to watch the colors pour forth from the sun,

the blue suit, the rooftops, and the big French bread!

Red Grooms. French Bread. 1963. Mixed media

Georgia O'Keeffe. Poppy. 1927. Oil on canvas

The Poppy of Georgia O'Keeffe

JANINE POMMY VEGA

In the carmine extravagance
the skirts of a Spanish dancer swirl
flamenco rhythms, castanets
exuberant dancer
drumming her heels on a wooden floor
staccato barks, deep intricate guitars
the energy pulsing from the dark
surrounds and enters

The poppy is wide open
her petals curve
like the skirts of a mountain
filled with the morning sun
we climb
and reaching the pinnacle shout
like the flower
in strict discipline, in eloquent satori
in the wild grace of black and red.

Diamante for Chuck

JAN GREENBERG

Ovals
Luminous, Hot
Popping, Pulsing, Swirling
Curlicues of Color, A Kaleidoscope
Blurring, Blending, Focusing
Immense, Intense
Self

Chuck Close, Self-Portrait, 1997. Oil on canvas.

Alfred Stieglitz. The Steerage. 1907. Chloride print

Steerage

The part of a passenger ship reserved for those traveling at the cheapest rate.

DAVID CITINO

A photograph can show us,
in color or in black and white,
what's wrong, what's right.

Look with me inside this ship.
We see, through the lens, a crowd
of families. It all looks loud,

though a photograph makes
noise only in our heads. Lives
are changing. Husbands, wives

and babies are sailing toward us,
who inhabit the future they desire,
free from poverty's dirty fire.

They sail in steerage, a mode
of going from dark to days
of light, to develop all the ways

of being themselves. The mast,
they hope, will grow into a leafy tree
and whisper, "Now you're free."

Jasper Johns. Map. 1961. Oil on canvas. © Jasper Johns/Licensed by VAGA, New York, NY

Map

J. PATRICK LEWIS

Brash canvas,
Bleeding borders,
Kindled calm,
This is oxymoronicamerica,
Forged out of iron and lace
By people strapping and raw,
Who wrestled and pinned history
To the map.

Happy as a circus boy,
Spirited as an outlaw,
Rough as a gandy dancer,
This continent of tinted steel
Spread an easel of colors
On fifty pieces of scissored history —
And painted itself a self.

EXPRESSIONS

Lessons from a Painting by Rothko

BOBBI KATZ

How would you paint a poem?
Prepare the canvas carefully
With tiers of misty rectangles
Stacked secrets waiting to be told.

Prepare the canvas carefully
With shallow pools of color
Stacked secrets waiting to be told
Messages from some unknown place

With shallow pools of color
Thin layers of gauze float over the
    canvas
Messages from some unknown place
Where soft shapes expand above
    a glow.

Thin layers of gauze float over the
    canvas
With tiers of misty rectangles
Where soft shapes expand above
    a glow.
How would you paint a poem?

Mark Rothko. **Untitled.** 1960. Oil on paper on canvas

On Lichtenstein's "Bananas & Grapefruit"

DEBORAH POPE

Roy Lichtenstein. **Bananas and Grapefruit #3.** 1972. Oil and magna on canvas

plump slump

slug plug

broke yolk

(hello

yellow!)

sealed in

unpeeled skin

gold fold

fruit suit

sluice of juices

squeezy teases

swelling lemon

jujubeezes

tipped ship *personification of banana*

nape shape

goo canoe

peel deal

rind grind

rough slough

slick lick

slow flow

squirt shirt

taste

haste

gulppulp

sweet part

eat

art

The Painting Comes Home

STEPHEN COREY

Charles Burchfield. **Six O'Clock.** 1936. Watercolor

So many paintings seem to be
　　somewhere else
in space and time: people are lost
　　in the background
or nowhere in sight, the buildings
　　are like foreign castles.

But here we have home and
　　suppertime,
the air on that edge between day
　　and evening,
the family gathered as the wall of
　　dark grows hard.

These bowed heads at the table
　　simply want food, then rest.
Because you know this place, you
　　can help them
find both. And because you are
　　strong you can lead them

outside to show them so much
　　more: the shadowed yard
whose rolling swells could be
　　waves, dunes, or even
　　mountains;
the six pointed roofs, each slightly
　　different,
lifting toward smoke or fog or
　　cloud;
and that moon, maybe sagging in
　　its lonely wish
to come down and join you, maybe
　　swelling tall
to light the yard and the house for
　　us all.

Joseph Stella. **Brooklyn Bridge: Variation on an Old Theme.** 1939.
Oil on canvas

River Song

WARREN WOESSNER

Crossing late is best,
The bridge strung
over the water
like a huge harp.
Sun caught
in the black strings
forms one pure note —
trembling,
falling as we rise,
reach out,
strain to hear
the perfect sound
that must be fading
just above our heads.

Girl Writing

JANE O. WAYNE

Milton Avery. **Girl Writing**. 1941. Oil on canvas

If you didn't stop in front of her,
you might only glimpse the target-red of socks,
and legs white as ropes, twined around each other.

You'd have to pause before you'd see
a girl staring at a desk, face flushed and eye-less,
her left-handed pen already at the bottom of the page.

From a foot away it looks easy — all of it —
just patches of pure color.
You'd think he took them straight out of their tubes

as we did crayons from a box —
paint smoothed on
the way a knife spreads mustard over bread.

Step back again and yes — the face is featureless,
the feet larger than the head, and one arm
bluer than the other.

Portrait maybe — since someone says his daughter
posed for it — but nothing one can quarrel with,
not a likeness to hold to the original.

Still how much life hides behind the lies the painter tells:
the too-pink face, the floating desk,
the letter that's never mailed.

Here in a quiet room that has no door to close,
the furniture won't wear out. No one will buy the table,
no one inherit the wooden bench and move away.

Mobile/Stabile

for Alexander Calder, 1898–1976

RONALD WALLACE

His hands were endlessly active,
fashioning his whimsical wire portraits
for everyone at the party, Paris, 1922.
And then there was his circus,
with its clowns and acrobats,
its tiny trapese artists, its
lion tamers and ambulance crew.
Innocence, the art critics said,
a world without guile or evil.
Of course, there were wars
and children — *What's that!*
he demanded when his daughter
showed him a crayoned thing or two.
Mobiles were his invention —
aluminum, steel, and light —

his planetary system. But then,
I love red so much, he said,
*that I almost want to paint everything
red.* And so he moved on to
stabiles! Huge, red, unpretentious
enough for Grand Rapids, Michigan
to emboss on their buses and garbage
trucks. And then he was dead.
And where does that leave us?
Strung out two decades later, up
too late at the century's party,
unwhimsical, tired, and wireless?
Or cockeyed, but perfectly balanced,
our hands across the blank paper
entranced by the emptiest wind!

Alexander Calder. Opposite: **Elephant and Trainer from Calder's Circus.** 1926–1931. Wood, cloth, rubber tubing, wire, fur, pipe cleaners, cork, and nails. Above: **La Grand Vitesse.** 1969. Steel plates, bolts, and paint

Pas de Trois

SANDY ASHER

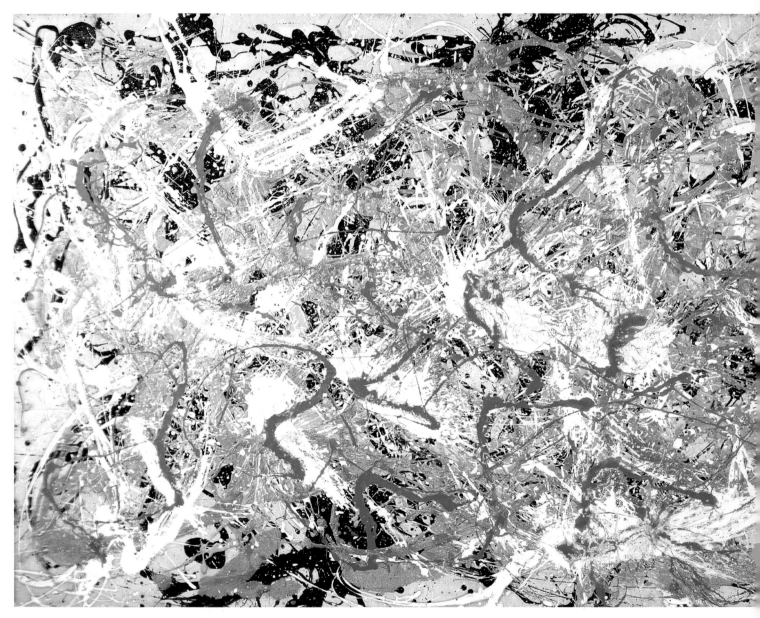

Jackson Pollock. **Number 27.** 1950. Oil on canvas

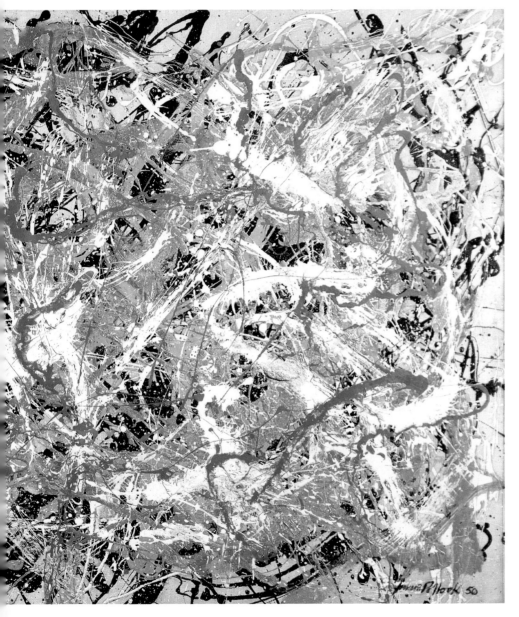

"You cannot,"
it's been said,
"separate the dancer
from the dance."

Sculptors
step away,
poets
put down their pens;
their work endures.

Hands
that pluck the strings
of a harp
are neither instrument
nor celestial song.

But no dance exists
without its dancer.

To my eye, this line
choreographs:
glissade,
arabesque,
tombé,
pirouette . . .
Strength, balance,
energy and rhythm
draw me in.
A dance is clearly intended.

Between us
appears
the dancer.

Man Ray Stares into the Future of Jazz: 1919

DAVID CLEWELL

Picture a quartet on the bandstand, drawn into
the colors of pure sound:
a whisper across a wet reed,
the age-old tension between drum and stick,
fingers just now touching down on the bass strings
and the keyboard, and maybe the moon, for all anyone knows
about this history on the edge of being made.
Someone's looking inside those black & white notes rising,
breaking free of their staves, swirling and jumping
and curling, coming back together in wave after wave —
towering sheets of music sure to turn the shape of jazz

inside out. And whoever listens to it will be utterly unstrung,
assuredly giddy in this unheard-of spectrum,
and no matter what they'll have planned for the rest of the day,
they're bound to find themselves suddenly improvising
all over the place. Later there will be time for Miles & Trane,
the Duke and the Count, Prez and Monk and Dizzy and Bird —
all the colorful names of jazz still to come —

but right now it's this offbeat cat Man Ray, from Philly
and, man, he's laying it down in those crazy, tinted shades
of gone yellow, gone orange, gone blue and green, and a few
there are no proper names for yet. He's blowing a cool breeze
of tempera and ink. He's stretching out, taking his solo
anywhere he likes the sound of. Clearly, he's seen
where the music is headed. He's heard something, and he's going
exquisitely on record, making a brilliant note of it.

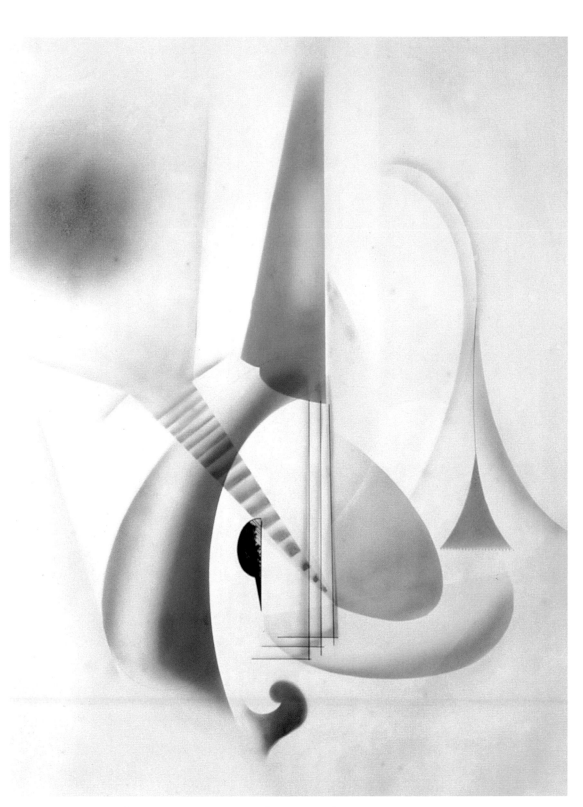

Man Ray. **Jazz**. c. 1919. Tempera and ink (aerograph)

More Light

DONALD FINKEL

He himself admitted that it might be present,
but denied that it was intended. Indeed, the
emphasis on it annoyed him: "The loneliness thing
is overdone," he said. But it undeniably exists.
— Lloyd Goodrich, *Edward Hopper*

Or is it the *light* that exists for him as he paints?
Not that old buttery-yellow light-bulb light,
but this miraculous light the makers call "fluorescent,"
this clear-as-day light that bathes the diner,
this harbor in a sea of darkness. How it pours
through the plate-glass window, rinsing the red brick
wall across the street, spilling through the window
of somebody fast asleep! It's seeping into her dream.

You'd think the man in the white cap had more light
than a man would need to make it through this night.
The coffee urns are beaming over his shoulder
like stainless angels! What else would he talk about
to the dude whose cigarette's gone out? And what
would the lady be studying there but a book of matches?
And the man in the dark grey hat with his back to us —
is there anything left in his glass but light, more light?

Edward Hopper. **Nighthawks.** 1942. Oil on canvas

Ladies and Gentlemen, Step Right Up, The Drawer Is Open!

HETTIE JONES

for Elizabeth, with love

Elizabeth Murray. **Open Drawer.** 1998. Oil on canvas

Look!   Out of the great green dresser of life

come   things with twisting strings —

                                    Catch!

                    that memory and desire
        before they hit the floor!

Is this the right drawer to open?

Is it the top?   As in   "You're Top Drawer, Baby"!

        But suppose the Top starts to

                            T
                        o
                            p
                        p
                            l
                        e

                and
        lets loose a torrent
                of red and spots and

        where's that yellow
            coming from?

What's to be done with our lives?   Oh —

                    Forever another surprise!

Florine Stettheimer. **The Cathedrals of Broadway.** 1920s. Oil on canvas

The World, Starring You

NAOMI SHIHAB NYE

Florine, we would live inside your colors! Red joy,
golden rushes of hope, the 1929 that we will never see.
Names of radiant theaters flame your sky — RIALTO — ROXY —
citizens mingling in pearls, top hats, inside a glittering flare.
Where have they gone? A ticket booth waits like a small domed mosque.
An usher — or is he a policeman? — wearing white gloves and yellow cape
pivots between welcome and EXIT. Even the mayor looks smart.
Frills and flags, banners, tiny dancing sprites . . .
You painted the flurry and flux,
abundant addresses of Broadway welcoming crowds.
I like the fanfare, the dreamy dazzle, canopies of light!

Florine, the early 20th century chimed like a chord,
but we are hobblers at the millennium, cleaning out our drawers,
nothing looks enough like you.
The age of gracious penmanship was yours.
Balance your globe on our tipsy clock,
lift the darkness with arches and stars.
And ever, ever, a roped-off fluted SILENCE at the center.
Take us where you were and where you are.

Biographical Notes on Poets

SANDY ASHER has written eighteen books for young readers and three dozen produced plays, including *A Woman Called Truth* and *Across the Plains.* Her many honors include the Charlotte Chorpenning Award for a body of work in children's theater. She lives in Springfield, Missouri, where she is Writer-in-Residence at Drury University.

MARVIN BELL has written seventeen books of poetry and related writings, including *Poetry for a Midsummer's Night* and *Wednesday.* Before deciding to concentrate on poetry, he was a musician, a photographer, and a potter. He lives in Iowa City, Iowa, where he teaches for the University of Iowa.

JACINTO JESÚS CARDONA is the author of *Pan Dulce,* a collection of poetry, and has published poems in a number of literary journals. He lives in San Antonio, Texas, where he teaches at Edgewood Communication and Fine Arts Academy. "*Bato,*" he says, "is a Spanglish greeting equivalent to 'Hey, man!' but it's also associated with *pachucos,* the alienated youth associated with zoot suiters."

SIV CEDERING has written eighteen books, including two novels, six books for children, and several collections of poetry, most recently *Letters from the Floating World.* A painter as well as an award-winning author, she lives in Long Island, New York, where she is working on an exhibition of poetry sculptures.

DEBORAH CHANDRA has written three books of poetry for children, including *Balloons and Other Poems* and *Miss Mabel's Table.* A recipient of the Lee Bennett Hopkins Poetry Award, she lives in southern California where she teaches third grade near the Los Angeles Arboretum, which is the home of many peacocks.

DAVID CITINO, a grandchild of immigrants from Italy, has written ten books of poetry, including *The Book of Appassionata* and *Broken Symmetry.*

He lives in Columbus, Ohio, where he teaches at Ohio State University and writes for the *Columbus Dispatch.*

DAVID CLEWELL has written seven collections of poetry, including *Blessings in Disguise,* a National Poetry Series winner, and *Now We're Getting Somewhere,* a Pollak Poetry Prize. He lives in Webster Groves, Missouri, where he teaches at Webster University. He says, "I once dreamed of setting the world on fire with my trumpet, but the world apparently had other ideas."

STEPHEN COREY has written seven collections of poetry, most recently, *Mortal Fathers and Daughters* and *All These Lands You Call One Country.* His work has appeared in such anthologies as *The Pushcart Prize* and *The Random House Book of Light Verse.* He lives in Athens, Georgia.

DAVE ETTER has written twenty-five books of poetry, most recently *Sunflower County* and *How High the Moon.* A recipient of the Carl Sandburg Award for *West of Chicago,* he lives in Lanark, Illinois.

DONALD FINKEL has written fifteen volumes of poetry, most recently *A Question of Seeing.* A recipient of the Theodore Roethke Memorial Award and a finalist of the National Book Award and the National Book Critics Circle Award, he was Poet in Residence at Washington University until 1991. He lives in St. Louis, Missouri.

KRISTINE O'CONNELL GEORGE has written three volumes of poetry for young readers, including *The Great Frog Race* and *Old Elm Speaks.* She has received the Lee Bennett Hopkins and the Myra Cohn Livingston poetry awards. She lives in Agoura, California, where she teaches children's poetry for the UCLA Writer's Program.

GARY GILDNER has written seventeen books, including *Blue Like the Heaven: New and Selected Poems,* a novel *The Second Bridge,* and a memoir about coaching a baseball team, *The Warsaw Sparks.* Among his awards are the

Pushcart Prize and the Theodore Roethke Memorial Award. He lives on a ranch in Idaho's Clearwater Mountains.

JAN GREENBERG has written thirteen books for young readers, most recently *Frank O. Gehry Outside In* (with Sandra Jordan). Among her honors are a *Boston Globe* Horn Book Honor Award for *Chuck Close Up Close* (with Sandra Jordan), as well as ten Best Book awards. The editor for this collection, she lives in St. Louis, Missouri.

JOY HARJO, a member of the Muscogee Nation, has published many books, including *A Map to the Next World* and *The Good Luck Cat.* She plays saxophone and performs her poetry with her band Poetic Justice. A recipient of the William Carlos Williams Award and the Lifetime Achievement Award from the Native Writers Circle of America, she lives in Honolulu, Hawaii.

DAVID HARRISON has written forty-eight poetry collections and picture books for young readers, including *When Cows Come Home, Wild Country,* and *The Boy With a Drum.* He is the recipient of many awards, such as the Christopher Award and the Bank Street College Book of the Year. He lives in Springfield, Missouri.

ANGELA JOHNSON has written twenty-two books for young readers, including picture books, a collection of poetry, *The Other Side,* and a novel, *Gone from Home.* A recipient of two Coretta Scott King Awards and the Lee Bennett Hopkins Poetry Award, she lives in Northeastern Ohio, but family ties in Alabama remain strong and inspire her work.

TONY JOHNSTON has written over one hundred books, including five poetry collections. Among her honors is the Once Upon A World Award in Children's Literature from the Simon Wiesenthal Museum for her book *The Wagon.* She lives in Southern California, where, she says, "The West is in my bones."

HETTIE JONES has written numerous books for children and adults, including *Drive,* a collection of poetry, which received the Norma Farber Award, *Five Women in Black Music,* and a memoir, *How I Became Hettie Jones.* Chair of the PEN Prison Writing Committee, she lives in New York City.

LAURA KASISCHKE has written a number of volumes of poetry, including *Fire and Flower* and *Wild Brides,* and a novel, *Suspicious River.* She lives in Chelsea, Michigan.

BOBBI KATZ has written over fifty books for children, including poetry, novels, picture books, and a biography. Her most recent poetry collections for young readers are *Listen: A Book of Noisy Poems* and *We, The People.* A former editor of children's books, she lives in New York City and Port Ewen, New York.

RON KOERTGE has written a number of award-winning novels for young adults and four collections of poetry, most recently *High School Dirty Poems* and *Life on the Edge of the Continent.* A recipient of grants from the California Arts Council and the National Endowment for the Arts, he lives in Pasadena, California, where he teaches at the city college.

X. J. KENNEDY has written many acclaimed books for children and adults, most recently *A Child's Introduction to Poetry* (with his wife Dorothy Kennedy). His books for young readers include *Brats, Uncle Switch,* and *Elympics.* A recipient of the Lamont Award for Poetry and the Aiken Taylor Award for Modern Poetry, he lives in Lexington, Massachusetts.

J. PATRICK LEWIS has written over thirty books for young people, including picture books and poetry, most recently *A Burst of Firsts, Freedom Like Sunlight,* and *Isabella Abnormella.* An economist, children's book reviewer, short story writer, and poet, he lives in Chagrin Falls, Ohio.

CONSTANCE LEVY has written four collections of poetry for young people. Her poems have received many honors, including the Lee Bennett Hopkins Honor Award for *A Crack in the Clouds* and the *Boston Globe* Horn Book Honor Award for *A Tree Place.* She lives in St. Louis, Missouri.

LYN LIFSHIN has written numerous volumes of poetry and has edited four anthologies of women's writing, including *Lips Unsealed.* Recent poetry collections include *Before It's Light, Cold Comfort,* and *Blue Tattoo.* An award-winning documentary, "Lyn Lifshin: Not Made of Glass," profiled her life and her work. She lives in Vienna, Virginia.

DAN MASTERSON has written four volumes of poetry, including *World Without End* and *All Things Seen and Unseen.* His awards include the Bullis Prize and two Pushcart Prizes. A director of poetry writing programs at both Rockland Community College and Manhattanville College, he lives in Pearl River, New York.

DAVID MURA is a poet, nonfiction writer, critic, playwright, and performance artist who has written five books, including *Turning Japanese: Memoirs of a Sansei.* His collection of poetry *The Colors of Desire* won the Carl Sandburg Literary Award and *After We Lost Our Way* won the National Poetry Series Contest. He lives in Minneapolis, Minnesota.

PETER F. NEUMEYER has written ten books for children and adults, including poetry, picture books, translations, and criticism. His most recent book for children is *The Annotated Charlotte's Web.* A children's book reviewer for the *Boston Globe* and other publications, he lives in Kensington, California.

NAOMI SHIHAB NYE has published twenty-four books for adults and children, including anthologies, a novel, essays, and poetry collections, most recently *Come With Me* and *Salting the Ocean: 100 Poems by Young Poets.* Among her honors were five Best Book awards for her novel for young readers, *Habibi,* and a Guggenheim Fellowship. A musician as well as a poet, she lives in San Antonio, Texas.

DEBORAH POPE is the author of five books, including three collections of poetry, *Fanatic Heart, Mortal World,* and *Falling Out of the Sky.* Her books have been nominated for the Pulitzer Prize and the National Book Award. She lives in Chapel Hill, North Carolina, where she is a professor at Duke University.

BRENDA SEABROOKE is the author of fifteen books for young readers, including two books of poetry, *Judy Scuppernong* and the sequel *Under the Pear Tree.* A recipient of the *Boston Globe* Horn Book Honor Award and many Notable awards, she recently moved to an island off Florida.

WILLIAM JAY SMITH, former Consultant in Poetry to the Library of Congress (now the Poet Laureate position), has published over fifty books for children and adults. His prize-winning children's verse is collected in *Laughing Time: Collected Nonsense.* Two of his collections of poetry were finalists for the National Book Award. He divides his time between Cummington, Massachusetts, and Paris, France.

ROBERT STEWART has written four books, including two collections of poetry. A winner of the PEN Syndicated Fiction Award, he recently edited (with Gloria Vando) *Spud Songs: An Anthology of Potato Poems* to benefit hunger relief. He credits his interest in tools to his father and grandfather, who were plumbers. He lives in Kansas City, Missouri.

SUSAN TERRIS is the author of numerous books for adults and young readers, including the novel *Nell's Quilt.* Among her collections of poetry are *Curved Space, Angels of Bataan,* and *Killing in the Comfort Zone.* A frequent contributor to poetry journals and anthologies, she lives in San Francisco, California.

LEE UPTON has written four books of poetry and three books of literary criticism. *Civilian History* is her most recent collection of poetry. She is a recipient of the Pushcart Prize and a winner of the National Poetry Series. She lives in Easton, Pennsylvania, where she teaches at Lafayette College.

JANINE POMMY VEGA has written fifteen books, including *Tracking the Serpent,* a book of travel, and most recently a collection of poetry, *Mad*

Dogs of Trieste. She performs around the country in English and Spanish with her band Tiamalu. A Director of Incisions /Arts, a group of writers working with people in prisons, she lives in Bearsville, New York.

RONALD WALLACE has written eleven books of poetry, fiction, and criticism, including *Quick Bright Things* and *The Uses of Adversity.* Among his many honors are the Helen Bullis Award and the Banta Award. Director of the creative writing program at the University of Wisconsin–Madison, he divides his time between Madison and a forty-acre farm in Bear Valley, Wisconsin.

JANE O. WAYNE is the author of *Looking Both Ways,* which won the Devins Prize for Poetry, and *A Strange Heart,* which won the Marianne Moore Poetry Prize and the Society of Midland Authors Poetry Prize. Her work has appeared in numerous journals and anthologies. She lives in St. Louis, Missouri.

CAROLE BOSTON WEATHERFORD has written six books for children, including *Sink or Swim: Black Lifesavers of the Outer Banks* and *Juneteenth Jamboree.* A recipient of the Furious Flower Poetry Prize, she lives in High Point, North Carolina. She chose to highlight the boxer Joe Louis because he "affirmed that African-Americans could overcome prejudice and attain greatness."

NANCY WILLARD has written numerous award-winning books for both children and adults, including *Pish Posh Said Hieronymous Bosch* and *The Tale I Told Sasha.* Among the books she has both written and illustrated are *An Alphabet for Angels* and *The Magic Cornfield.* She received the John Newbery Medal for *A Visit to William Blake's Inn: Poems for Innocent and Experienced Travelers.* She lives in Poughkeepsie, New York.

WARREN WOESSNER has written six volumes of poetry, most recently *Storm Lines* and *Iris Rising.* Among his honors is a National Endowment for the Arts Fellowship. A founder of *Abraxas* magazine, he lives in Minneapolis, Minnesota, where he is a patent attorney in biotechnology.

JANET S. WONG has written eight books for young readers, including two award-winning volumes of poetry, *Good Luck Gold* and *A Suitcase of Seaweed,* both accounts of the Asian-American experience. Her most recent books for children include *The Trip Back Home* and *This Next New Year.* A former lawyer who gave up practicing law to write for young people, she lives in Medina, Washington.

JANE YOLEN, a storyteller, poet, novelist, and playwright, is the author of over two hundred books for children and adults. Her many awards include the Caldecott Medal, the Golden Kite Award, and the Christopher Medal. Her most recent titles are *How Does a Dinosaur Say Goodnight?* and *Sister Emily's Lightship.* She divides her time between Hatfield, Massachusetts, and St. Andrew's, Scotland.

Biographical Notes on Artists

PACITA ABAD (b. 1946), born on a remote island in the Philippines, calls her work "Trapunto Paintings," after the technique of stitching and stuffing fabric developed in Italy in the fourteenth century. Six large-scale trapunto paintings called *Masks from Six Continents* can be seen at a Metro station in Washington D.C., where she resides.

MILTON AVERY (1893–1965), born in New York, is considered one of America's great colorists, who, in his poetic works, strove to eliminate detail and to simplify shape and line. His work influenced the American color imagists of the 1960s, such as Mark Rothko.

ROMARE BEARDEN (1912–1988), born in North Carolina, celebrated African-American culture through his paintings. He also portrayed the effects of racism and poverty, which he brought to the public's attention in the 1930s and 1940s. His collages, made in New York City and the Caribbean, chronicle the black experience as he lived it.

GEORGE WESLEY BELLOWS (1882–1925), born in Ohio, worked in New York, where he gained great popularity for his dynamic paintings of ordinary life. An artist who represented the restless spirit of America in his work, he enjoyed painting people, especially prizefighters and his family.

THOMAS HART BENTON (1889–1975), who lived in New York and later returned to Missouri, where he was born, championed regionalism in his paintings of everyday life. His twisting figures and landscapes are charged with energy and movement.

LOUISE BOURGEOIS (b. 1911), one of America's distinguished sculptors, was born in Paris. A master stone carver, she works in many other mediums as well. In recent years, her installation pieces, including *Le Defi,* have been exhibited throughout the world to great critical acclaim. She lives in New York City.

CHARLES BURCHFIELD (1893–1967), born in Ohio, lived in Buffalo, New York, where he painted scenes of urban and small-town life, as well as landscapes. Although he did many paintings in oils, he was particularly fond of watercolor. His studies of houses have a peculiarly lifelike, almost eerie quality.

ALEXANDER CALDER (1898–1976), born in Philadelphia, worked primarily in Paris, France, and New York. He invented the mobile, an abstract sculptural form constructed of wire and metal discs, set into motion by air drafts. He became famous in the 1920s for his circus animals and performers created from materials such as cork, wood, and wire, called *Calder's Circus*.

CHRISTO (b. 1935), born in Bulgaria, and **JEANNE-CLAUDE (b. 1935)**, born in Casablanca, met in Paris in 1957, where they did their first "wrapped" pieces. Since then, they have done large-scale wrapped projects all over the world. At sunrise in 1991, 1,880 workers opened the 3,100 umbrellas in Ibaraki, Japan, and California. The installation lasted for eighteen days.

CHUCK CLOSE (b. 1940) grew up in Tacoma, Washington. His large photorealistic paintings in black and white, portraits of friends and family, were first shown in New York City in 1967. He continues to paint portraits from Polaroids, filling a blank gridded surface with a kaleidoscope of brushstrokes, out of which the "head" of his subject comes into focus.

STUART DAVIS (1894–1964), born in Philadephia, was stimulated by the sights and sounds of New York City and the Jazz Age. His paintings are filled with colorful signs and symbols of America on the move. His innovative paintings from the 1920s through the 1950s incorporated both abstract and realistic forms and influenced modern advertising styles.

JIM DINE (b. 1935), born in Ohio, works in both New York and Vermont. A painter and a sculptor, he has been identified with the Pop Art movement for his use of everyday objects in his work. A major figure in contemporary art, he has been widely exhibited both in the United States and Europe.

ARTHUR DOVE (1880–1946) lived most of his life in upstate New York and on Long Island. He is considered America's first abstract painter, whose style was based on emotions and derived from nature. Dove emphasized the elements of art in his painting — color, line, shape, and texture — rather than concentrating on imitating reality.

RED GROOMS (b. 1937), a painter and filmmaker, was born in Nashville, Tennessee. He is well-known for his large constructions of cutout figures and

objects painted in bright colors that satirize the American scene, such as *Ruckus Rodeo* and *Ruckus Manhattan*.

EDWARD HOPPER (1882–1967), who lived in New York City and Cape Cod, Massachusetts, captured the experience of loneliness and isolation Americans felt as the country changed from a rural to an urban society. His powerful psychological studies of people and places are considered classics of American painting.

JASPER JOHNS (b. 1930), born in North Carolina, moved to New York City in 1952. His early paintings of flags and targets changed our conventional way of viewing these well-known symbols. His works were largely responsible for deflecting the course of Abstract Expressionism and paved the way for Pop Art.

WILLIAM H. JOHNSON (1901–1970), who grew up in South Carolina, went to New York City in 1918 and became a leading member of a movement of African-American poets, artists, and musicians known as the Harlem Renaissance. He traveled all over the world, from New York to North Africa and Europe, to live and to paint his colorful images of everyday life.

JACOB LAWRENCE (1917–2000) grew up in Harlem in New York City. His paintings are often social commentaries on African-American life. His works are characterized by stylized figures in strong colors and flattened patterns.

ROY LICHTENSTEIN (1923–1997), associated with the Pop Art movement, was born and lived in New York City. Using thick black lines and the Benday dot patterns of commercial printing, he reproduced images from comic strips, as well as adapted the work of other artists. His work explores the formal issues of painting and the ironies of contemporary culture.

ERIC LINDBLOOM (b. 1934), born in Detroit, Michigan, is a photographer who lives in Poughkeepsie, New York. His monograph *Angels of the Arno*, photographs of Florence, Italy, was published in 1994. Exclusively printed in black and white, his photography, which has been exhibited in the

United States and Japan, evokes a deep awareness of the environment.

MAN RAY (1890–1976), referred to as a Dadaist and Surrealist artist because of his interest in dreams and the unconscious mind, was born in Philadelphia, Pennsylvania, but lived on and off in Paris, France, and New York City. His early paintings were abstract. Later, he turned to making objects assembled out of a variety of incongruous parts.

MARISOL (b. 1930), born in Paris of Venezuelan parents, moved to New York City in 1950. Her work, often consisting of life-sized figures made of blocks of wood meticulously decorated with paint and other materials, offers a satiric look at contemporary life.

CÉSAR A. MARTÍNEZ (b. 1944) was born in Larado, Texas, to immigrant parents from Mexico. His work deals with the concerns of contemporary Chicano culture and has been widely exhibited in museums both nationally and internationally, most recently at a retrospective at the McNay Art Museum in San Antonio, Texas, where he lives.

BARBARA MORGAN (1900–1992), a painter and photographer, grew up in Southern California and moved to New York City in 1930. Admired as a portraitist, she specialized in black-and-white photographs of dance, which she defined as "the life force in action." A pioneer of photomontage, she also owned a photographic publishing house.

Anna Mary Robertson Moses, known as **GRANDMA MOSES (1860–1961)** was a self-taught artist from Eagle Bridge, New York, who began painting at the age of seventy-seven. An American folk painter, she chose her subject matter from the historical past of the rural area in which she lived, and her work celebrated the routine activities of farm life.

ELIZABETH MURRAY (b. 1940), born in Chicago, is well known for her painted reliefs, three-dimensional shaped canvases. At first glance, they seem abstract, but they often depict intimate domestic objects with a feminist theme. Her work has been widely exhibited in New York City, where she lives, and internationally.

ELIE NADELMAN (1882–1946), a sculptor, was born in Poland and fled Europe with the outbreak of World War I in 1914 to the United States. Some of his most famous sculptures, such as *Woman at the Piano,* echo the simplicity of American folk art, which he and his wife collected.

GEORGIA O'KEEFFE (1887–1986) was born in Wisconsin but spent most of her life in New York and New Mexico. Her unique paintings, which vibrate with color, were inspired by subjects such as flowers, buildings, and the desert. Fiercely independent and strong-minded, she is considered one of the leading figures of American modernism.

JACKSON POLLOCK (1912–1956), born in Wyoming, moved to New York in the 1940's and took the art world by storm. His painting technique, created by dripping, pouring, and splattering paint as he moved around the canvas, is known as Abstract Expressionism. This movement was instrumental in moving the center of art from Paris, France, to New York City.

FAITH RINGGOLD (b. 1930), who grew up in Harlem in New York City, is best known for her painted story quilts, an art form that combines storytelling, painting, and quilted fabric. She has exhibited in major museums around the world. Her first illustrated book, *Tar Beach,* won a Caldecott Honor award.

MARK ROTHKO (1903–1970), born in Russia, grew up in Oregon and later moved to New York City. His abstract paintings of soft rectangles have an atmospheric, spiritual quality that immerse the viewer in color and light. Considered a leading Abstract Expressionist, he produced sensuous canvases, which are exhibited in many public collections.

CHARLES M. RUSSELL (1864–1926), cowboy artist and recorder of the Old West, was born in St. Louis, Missouri, but moved to Montana to live and work. Self-taught, he was a painter, printmaker, and sculptor, well known for his studies of the people and animals of the west.

JAUNE QUICK-TO-SEE SMITH (b. 1940) was born in Montana and raised on the Flatland Reservation. Deeply connected to her heritage, her works in paint and mixed media address the myths of her ancestors in the context of current issues facing Native Americans.

KIKI SMITH (b. 1954), born in Germany, is a contemporary sculptor and printmaker whose art concerns the fragility of the human body. Her sculpture, often of fragmented body parts, has a disturbing quality, as well as a distinct feminist intention. A critically acclaimed artist, she works in New York City.

FRANK STELLA (b. 1936), born in Massachusetts, moved to New York City in the 1950s. His first Minimalist paintings were orderly and monochromatic. Later, he went on to paint large, shaped canvases in bright colors and geometric shapes. His recent works, incorporating painted metal in wild patterns and forms, have become more complex and less formal.

JOSEPH STELLA (1877–1946), a painter, lived in New York City. He produced paintings in a variety of styles, two of which are represented here. His earlier semi-abstract paintings of figures and still-lifes, such as *The Peacock,* have a dreamy, exotic quality. His more geometric series of the Brooklyn Bridge are landmarks of American modernism.

FLORINE STETTHEIMER (1871–1944), a painter of independent imagination, chose to exhibit only once in New York City. There she presided over a famous salon for artists in the 1920s. Although she was a trained artist, her naive technique and pastel palette gave her work an innocent quality. Her use of Americana influenced artists in the 1960s.

ALFRED STIEGLITZ (1864–1945), photographer, editor, and art gallery director, was born in New Jersey, studied in Europe, and moved to New York City. He established an important gallery for avant-garde art in 1905. He championed both American photographers and artists, including Arthur Dove and Georgia O'Keeffe (to whom he was later married).

ANDY WARHOL (1928–1987), painter and filmmaker, was born in Pittsburgh, Pennsylvania, and moved to New York City in the 1950s. His cool, ironic paintings of popular culture, from soup cans to movie stars, silkscreened onto the canvas, earned him the title of America's most celebrated Pop artist.

GRANT WOOD (1892–1941), who was born on a farm in Iowa, painted witty, meticulously detailed paintings of the American heartland. He was considered a political and social radical in Iowa, but elsewhere he was categorized as a regionalist painter, along with Thomas Hart Benton, for his celebration of the values of midwestern life.

PHOTOGRAPH CREDITS: **PAGE 7:** Thomas Hart Benton. *Down by the Riverside.* 1969. Oil on canvas, 19 × 23″ (45.6 × 58.42 cm). Private Collection. © T. H. Benton and R. P. Benton Testamentary Trusts / Licensed by VAGA, New York, NY. **PAGE 8:** Elie Nadelman. *Woman at the Piano.* c. 1917. Wood, stained and painted, 35⅛ × 23¼ × 9″ (89.2 × 59.1 × 22.9 cm), including base. The Museum of Modern Art, New York. The Philip L. Goodwin Collection. Photograph © 1999 The Museum of Modern Art, New York. **PAGE 9:** Joseph Stella. *The Peacock.* c. 1919. Pastel on paper, 25¼ × 18¼″ (61.86 × 44.71 cm). Collection of Mr. and Mrs. Richard A. Lippe. Photograph courtesy of Richard York Gallery, New York, NY. **PAGE 10:** Eric Lindbloom. *Horses.* 1979. Gelatin silver print, 7½ × 7½″ (19.05 × 19.05 cm). Courtesy of Gallery 292, New York, NY. **PAGE 11:** Charles M. Russell. *Animal Figurine "Buffalo."* 1900–20. Bronze sculpture 4½ × 6¼ × 3⅝″ (11.59 × 15.89 × 9.20 cm). Autry Museum of Western Heritage, Los Angeles. **PAGE 12:** William H. Johnson. *Joe Louis and Unidentified Boxer.* 1939–42. Tempera, pen, and ink with pencil on paper, 18 × 12″ (45.72 × 30.48 cm). National Museum of American Art, Smithsonian Institution, Gift of the Harmon Foundation. **PAGE 13:** César A. Martínez. *Bato Con Khakis.* 1982. Mixed media on paper. Collection: Joe A. Diaz, San Antonio, Texas. **PAGES 14–15:** Edward Hopper. *Early Sunday Morning.* 1930. Oil on canvas. $35\frac{3}{16}$ × 60¼″ (89.4 × 153 cm). Collection of Whitney Museum of American Art. Purchase, with funds from Gertrude Vanderbilt Whitney. Photograph © 1999 Whitney Museum of American Art. **PAGE 16:** Romare Bearden. *Black Manhattan.* 1969. Collage of paper and synthetic polymer paint on composition board, 22½ × 18″ (57⅕ × 45.72 cm). Schomberg Center for Research in Black Culture, The New York Public Library: Gift of Mr. and Mrs. Theodore Kheel. © Romare Bearden Foundation / Licensed by VAGA, New York, NY. **PAGE 17:** Stuart Davis. *Premiere.* 1957. Oil on canvas, 58 × 50″ (147.32 × 127 cm). Los Angeles County Museum of Art, Museum Purchase, Museum Art Council. © Estate of Stuart Davis / Licensed by VAGA, New York, NY. **PAGE 18:** Jim Dine. *The Crommelynck Gate with Tools.* 1984. Cast Bronze with welded appendages, 108 × 132 × 36″ (274.3 × 335.2 × 91.6 cm). The Nelson-Atkins Museum of Art, Kansas City, Missouri (Gift of the Friends of Art). **PAGE 19:** Arthur Dove. *That Red One.* 1944. Oil and wax on canvas, 27 × 36″ (68.6 × 91.4 cm). Museum of Fine Arts, Boston, MA. Gift of the William H. Lane Foundation. **PAGE 20:** Christo and Jeanne-Claude. *The Umbrellas, Japan–USA.* 1984–91. Ibaraki, Japan Site. Photographs by Wolfgang Volz. © Christo, 1991. **PAGE 21:** Christo and Jeanne-Claude. *The Umbrellas, Japan–USA.* 1984–91. California Site. Photographs by Wolfgang Volz. © Christo, 1991. **PAGE 22:** George Bellows. *Stag at Sharkey's.* 1909. Oil on canvas, 35⅞ × 47⅞″ (92 × 122.6 cm). © The Cleveland Museum of Art, 1999, Hinman B. Hurlbut Collection. **PAGE 25:** Faith Ringgold. *Tar Beach.* 1988. Acrylic on canvas bordered with printed, painted, quilted, and pieced cloth, 74⅝ × 68½″ (189.5 × 174 cm). Solomon R. Guggenheim Museum, New York. Gift, Mr. and Mrs. Gus and Judith Lieber, 1988. Photograph by David Heald © The Solomon R. Guggenheim Foundation, New York. **PAGE 26:** Pacita Abad. *How Mali Lost Her Accent.* 1991. Acrylic, oil, and collage on stitched and padded canvas, 97 × 70″ (246.4 × 177.8 cm). Courtesy of the Artist. **PAGE 28:** Barbara Morgan. *Martha Graham, Letter to the World (Kick).* 1940. Gelatin silver print, 14¾ × 18⅜″ (37.4 × 46.7 cm). The Museum of Modern Art, New York. John Spencer Fund. Copy Print © 1999 The Museum of Modern Art, New York. **PAGE 29:** Louise Bourgeois. *Defiance (Le Defi).* 1991. Painted wood, glass, and electric light, 67½ × 58 × 26″ (171.5 × 147.3 × 66 cm). Solomon R. Guggenheim Museum, New York. Photograph by David Heald © The Solomon R. Guggenheim Foundation, New York. Art © Louise Bourgeois / Licensed by VAGA, New York, NY. **PAGE 30:** Marisol. *The Family.* 1962. Painted wood and other materials in three sections, overall 6′10⅝″ × 65½″ × 15½″ (209.8 × 166.3 × 39.3 cm). The Museum of Modern Art, New York. Advisory Committee Fund. Photograph © 1999 The Museum of Modern Art, New York. Art © Marisol / Licensed by VAGA, New York, NY. **PAGE 32:** Andy Warhol. *Marilyn Diptych.* 1962. Synthetic polymer paint and silkscreen ink on canvas, 6′10″ × 57″ (208.28 × 144⅞ cm). © The Andy Warhol Foundation for the Visual Arts / Artists Rights Society (ARS), NY. Tate Gallery, London, Great Britain. **PAGE 34:** Jacob Lawrence. *Barber Shop.* 1946. Gouache on paper, 21⅛ × 29⅜″ (53.6 × 74.6 cm). The Toledo Museum of Art, Toledo, Ohio; Purchased with funds from the Library Endowment, Gift of Edward Drummond Library. **PAGE 35:** Jaune Quick-to-See Smith. *Indian, Indio, Indigenous.* 1992. Oil and collage on canvas, 60 × 100″ (152.4 × 254 cm). The National Museum of Women in the Arts, Museum Purchase: Members' Acquisition Fund. **PAGE 37:** Georgia O'Keeffe. *Red Hills and Bones.* 1941. Oil on canvas, 30 × 40″ (76.2 × 101.6 cm). Philadelphia Museum of Art: The Alfred Stieglitz Collection. © 2001 The Georgia O'Keeffe Foundation / Artists Rights Society (ARS), New York. **PAGE 38:** Grandma Moses. *Wash Day.* 1945. Oil on masonite, 17¾ × 23½″ (45 × 6.35 cm). Museum of Art, Rhode Island School of Design, Providence, RI. Gift of Mrs. Murray S. Danforth. © 1946 (renewed 1974). Grandma Moses Properties Co., New York. **PAGE 39:** Grant Wood. *American Gothic.* 1930. Oil on beaverboard, 29⅞ × 24⅞″ (74.3 × 62.4 cm). Friends of American Art Collection. All rights reserved by The Art Institute of Chicago and VAGA, New York, NY. Photograph © 1999, The Art Institute of Chicago. All Rights Reserved. **PAGES 40–41:** Frank Stella. *Madinat as Salam III.* 1971. Acrylic on canvas, 120 × 300″ (304.8 × 762 cm). Saint Louis Art Museum. Gift of Lawrence H. Greenberg, Mr. and Mrs. Robert G. Greenberg, and Mr. and Mrs. Ronald K. Greenberg. © 2001 Frank Stella / Artists Rights Society (ARS), New York. **PAGE 42:** Kiki Smith. *Untitled (Fluttering Eyes).* 1990. Silkscreen 29½ × 20½″ (74.93 × 52.07 cm). © 1994 Barbara Krakow Gallery. **PAGE 45:** Red Grooms. *French Bread.* 1963. Mixed media, 52 × 37″ (132.08 × 93.98 cm). Private Collection. © 2001 Red Grooms / Artists Rights Society (ARS), New York. Photograph courtesy of Marlborough Gallery, New York. **PAGE 46:** Georgia O'Keeffe. *Poppy.* 1927. Oil on canvas, 30 × 36″ (76.2 × 91.44 cm). Museum of Fine Arts, St. Petersburg, Florida. Gift of Charles and Margaret Stevenson Henderson in memory of Jeanne Crawford Henderson. **PAGE 49:** Chuck Close. *Self-Portrait.* 1997. Oil on canvas, 102 × 84″ (259.08 × 213.36 cm). Photograph by Ellen Page Wilson, courtesy of PaceWildenstein. **PAGE 50:** Alfred Stieglitz. *Steerage.* 1907. Chloride print, 4¼ × 3⅜″ (11 × 9.2 cm). Alfred Stieglitz Collection. Photograph courtesy of The Art Institute of Chicago. **PAGES 52–53:** Jasper Johns. *Map.* 1961. Oil on canvas, 6′6″ × 10′3⅛″ (198.2 × 314.7 cm). The Museum of Modern Art, New York. Gift of Mr. and Mrs. Robert C. Scull. © Jasper Johns / Licensed by VAGA, New York, NY. Photograph © 1999 The Museum of Modern Art, New York. **PAGE 55:** Mark Rothko. *Untitled.* 1960. Oil on canvas, 24 × 18″ (60.96 × 45.72 cm). Private Collection. © 2001 Kate Rothko Prizel and Christopher Rothko / Artists Rights Society (ARS), New York. **PAGE 56:** Roy Lichtenstein. *Bananas and Grapefruit #3.* 1972. Oil and magna on canvas, 28 × 40″ (71.12 × 101.6 cm). Private Collection. © Estate of Roy Lichtenstein. **PAGE 58:** Charles Burchfield. *Six O'Clock.* 1936. Watercolor, 24 × 30″ (61 × 76.2 cm). Collection of Everson Museum of Art, Syracuse, NY; Museum Purchase, Jennie Dickson Buck Fund. **PAGE 59:** Joseph Stella. *Brooklyn Bridge: Variation on an Old Theme.* 1939. Oil on canvas. 70 × 42″ (177.8 × 106.7 cm). Collection of Whitney Museum of American Art, New York. Photograph © 1999 Whitney Museum of American Art. **PAGE 60:** Milton Avery. *Girl Writing.* 1941. Oil on canvas, 48 × 32⅛″ (121.92 × 81.91 cm). Courtesy of The Phillips Collection, Washington, D.C. © 2001 Milton Avery Trust / Artists Rights Society (ARS), New York. **PAGE 62:** Alexander Calder. *Elephant and Trainer from Calder's Circus.* 1926–31. Wood, cloth, rubber tubing, wire, fur, pipe cleaners, cork, and nails. 12¼ × 29 × 15½ in. (31.1 × 73.7 × 39.4 cm). Collection of Whitney Museum of American Art, New York. Purchase, with funds from a public fundraising campaign in May 1982. One half the funds were contributed by the Robert Wood Johnson Jr. Charitable Trust. Additional major donations were given by the Lauder Foundation; the Robert Lehman Foundation, Inc.; the Howard and Jean Lipman Foundation, Inc.; an anonymous donor; The T.M. Evans Foundation, Inc.; MacAndrews & Forbes Group, Incorporated; the DeWitt Wallace Fund, Inc.; Martin and Agneta Gruss; Anne Phillips; Mr. and Mrs. Laurence S. Rockefeller; the Simon Foundation, Inc.; Marylou Whitney; Bankers Trust Company; Mr. and Mrs. Kenneth N. Dayton; Joel and Anne Ehrenkranz; Irvin and Kenneth Feld; Flora Whitney Miller. More than 500 individuals from 26 states and abroad also contributed to the campaign. **PAGE 63:** Alexander Calder. *La Grand Vitesse.* 1969. Steel plates, bolts, and paint, 516 × 660 × 300″ (1,463 × 1,676.4 × 762 cm). City of Grand Rapids, Chris Grey. **PAGES 64–65:** Jackson Pollock. *Number 27.* 1950. Oil on canvas. 49 × 106″ (124.5 × 269.2 cm). Collection of Whitney Museum of American Art, New York. © 2001 Pollock-Krasner Foundation / Artists Rights Society (ARS), New York. Photograph © 1999 Whitney Museum of American Art. **PAGE 67:** Man Ray. *Jazz.* 1919. Tempera and ink (aerograph), 28 × 22″ (71.12 × 55.88 cm). Courtesy, Columbus Museum of Fine Art, OH: Gift of Ferdinand Howald. © 2001 Man Ray Trust / Artists Rights Society, NY / ADAGP, Paris. **PAGES 68–69:** Edward Hopper. *Nighthawks.* 1942. Oil on canvas, 32¾ × 59½″ (84.1 × 152.4 cm). Friends of American Art Collection. Photograph © 1999, The Art Institute of Chicago. All Rights Reserved. **PAGE 70:** Elizabeth Murray. *Open Drawer.* 1998. Oil on canvas 9′4″ × 9′ (284 × 274 cm). © Elizabeth Murray. Photograph by Ellen Page Wilson, courtesy of PaceWildenstein. **PAGE 72:** Florine Stettheimer. *The Cathedrals of Broadway.* 1929. Oil on canvas, 60⅛ × 50⅛″ (152.72 × 127.32 cm). The Metropolitan Museum of Art, Gift of Ettie Stettheimer, 1953. Photograph © 1980 The Metropolitan Museum of Art.

POETRY CREDITS: "Down by the Riverside" © 2001 by Dave Etter; "Woman at the Piano" © 2001 by William Jay Smith; "The Peacock" © 2001 by Deborah Chandra; "Dream Horses" © 2001 by Nancy Willard; "The Bison Returns" © 2001 by Tony Johnston; "The Brown Bomber" © 2001 by Carole Boston Weatherford; "Bato Con Khakis" © 2001 by Jacinto Jesús Cardona; "Early Sunday Morning" © 2001 by Dan Masterson; "Sit a While" © 2001 by Siv Cedering; "Stuart Davis: Premier, 1957" © 2001 by X. J. Kennedy; "Crommelynck Gate" © 2001 by Robert Stewart; "A Word" © 2001 by Gary Gildner; "Dropped and Sprung" © 2001 by Janet S. Wong; "Ringside" © 2001 by Ron Koertge; "From Above" © 2001 by Angela Johnson; "Fresh from the Island Angel" © 2001 by David Mura; "Martha Graham in 'Letter to the World'" © 2001 by Lyn Lifshin; "A Provocation" © 2001 by Lee Upton; "Breaking Away from the Family" © 2001 by Susan Terris; "It's Me!" © 2001 by David Harrison; "America Talks" © 2001 by Peter F. Neumeyer; "Naming: Or, There is no such thing as an Indian" © 2001 by Joy Harjo; "Red Hills and Bones" © 2001 by Laura Kasischke; "On a Windy Wash Day Morn" © 2001 by Brenda Seabrooke; "Grant Wood: American Gothic" © 2001 by Jane Yolen; "Madinat as Salam" © 2001 by Constance Levy; "Pantoum for These Eyes" © 2001 by Kristine O'Connell George; "Big French Bread" © 2001 by Marvin Bell; "The Poppy of Georgia O'Keeffe" © 2001 by Janine Pommy Vega; "Diamante for Chuck" © 2001 by Jan Greenberg; "Steerage" © 2001 by David Citino; "Map" © 2001 by J. Patrick Lewis; "Lessons from a Painting by Rothko" © 2001 by Bobbi Katz; "On Lichtenstein's 'Bananas & Grapefruit'" © 2001 by Deborah Pope; "The Painting Comes Home" © 2001 by Stephen Corey; "River Song" © 2001 by Warren Woessner; "Girl Writing" © 2001 by Jane O. Wayne; "Mobile/Stabile" © 2001 by Ronald Wallace; "Pas de Trois" © 2001 by Sandy Asher; "Man Ray Stares into the Future of Jazz: 1919" © 2001 by David Clewell; "More Light" © 2001 by Donald Finkel; "Ladies and Gentelmen, Step Right Up, The Drawer Is Open!" © 2001 by Hettie Jones; "The World, Starring You" © 2001 by Naomi Shihab Nye.

Index

Entries in *italics* refer to illustrations.